# EVERYBODY HAS FEELINGS

# Everybody Has Feelings

Jon Burgerman

OXFORD

UNIVERSITY PRESS

Mitton      Pim      Mattie      Pokpok      Gruff

# Everybody has feelings.
# That's okay.

Gooey      Risa      Xav      Miyo      Bimlar      Nacho

Pawe    Khaim    Phoenix    Fluffy    Brompton

# How are YOU feeling today?

Hersy    Custard    Agugu    Sparkle    Humpfry

I feel JOYFUL. I like playing outside.

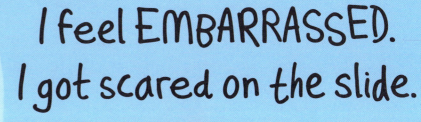

I feel EMBARRASSED.
I got scared on the slide.

I feel EXCITED.
There's so much to do.

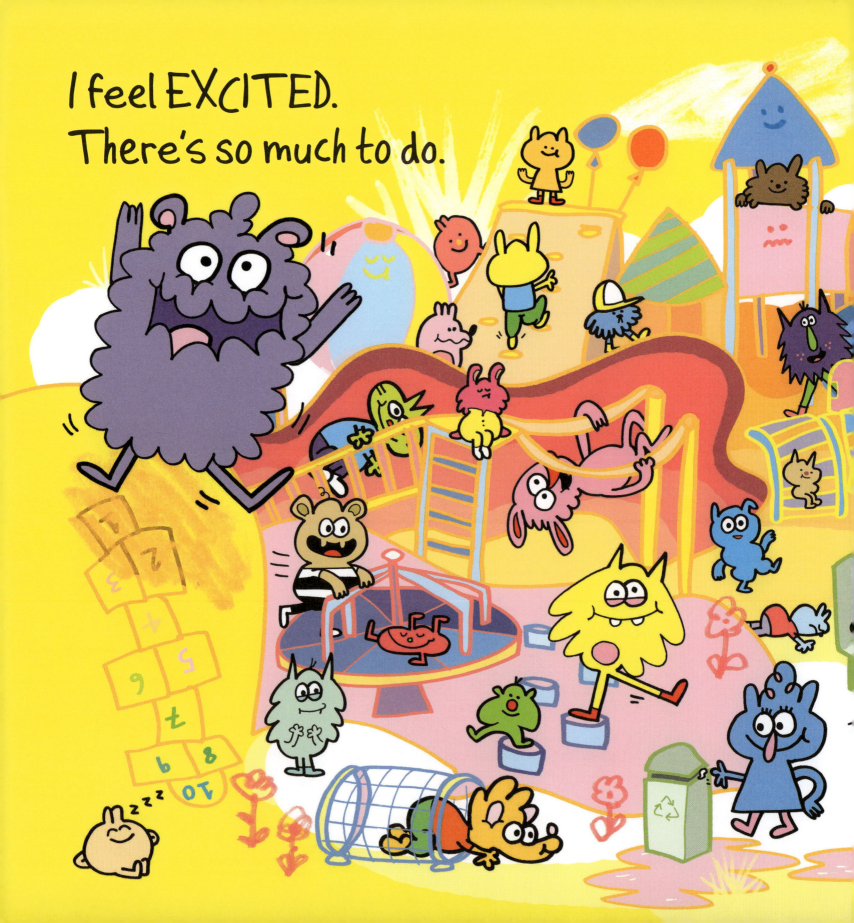

I feel FRUSTRATED. I can't tie my shoe.

I feel LOVED.
Our friendship has grown.

I feel BRAVE. I gave it a try!

I feel JEALOUS.
I want a skateboard.

I feel SHY.
I'm about to perform.

I feel CALM.
I'm cosy
and warm.

I feel CONFIDENT. I know how to skate.

I feel STRESSED. I just can't wait!

I feel KIND. Let's share these about.

I feel INSPIRED. I love the park.

I feel TIRED. It's getting dark.

I feel complete.

I feel like I ate too much sugar.

I feel lucky to have such generous friends.

I feel energised.

I feel proud of myself for sharing my feelings.

Sharing our feelings is good to do. Listening to each other is important too.

I'm not sure how I feel...

I feel ready for a nap.

I feel happy you read this book!

I feel I should be nicer to geese.

I feel okay, we all get scared sometimes.

You don't have to smile when you don't feel like it.

I feel talking about my feelings helped me.

It's okay to feel sad sometimes.

Let me know if you need a hug.

Feelings change all the time.

We all have feelings and that's okay! How are YOU feeling today?

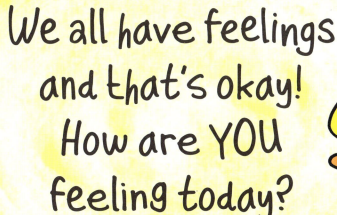

We're here for you!

If you can't say how you feel, maybe you can draw how you feel?

Feelings inspire how I express myself.

Friends listen to friends' feelings!

We love you!

This book is dedicated
to Esther and Aaron

# OXFORD
UNIVERSITY PRESS

Great Clarendon Street, Oxford OX2 6DP
Oxford University Press is a department of the University
of Oxford.It furthers the University's objective of excellence in
research, scholarship,and education by publishing worldwide.
Oxford is a registered trade mark of Oxford University Press
in the UK and in certain other countries

Text and Illustrations © Jon Burgerman 2020

The moral rights of the author and illustrator have been asserted
Database right Oxford University Press (maker)

First published 2021

British Library Cataloguing in Publication Data

Data available

ISBN: 978-0-19-276604-5

1 3 5 7 9 10 8 6 4 2

Main text set in Burgerman 1.7
with the permission of the author

Printed in China

Paper used in the production of this book
is a natural, recyclable product made
from wood grown in sustainable forests.
The manufacturing process
conforms to the environmental
regulations of the country of origin.